THIS LAND CALLED AMERICA: NORTH CAROLINA

C

CREATIVE EDUCATION

Published by Creative Education
P.O. Box 227, Mankato, Minnesota 56002
Creative Education is an imprint of The Creative Company
www.thecreativecompany.us

Design by Blue Design (www.bluedes.com)
Art direction by Rita Marshall
Book production by The Design Lab
Printed in the United States of America

Photographs by Alamy (John Elk III, Andre Jenny), Corbis (Bettmann, CNP, Brownie Harris, Randy Lincks, David Muench, Michael Nicholson, Richard T. Nowitz, Ellen Ozier/Reuters, Richard Hamilton Smith, G.E. Kidder Smith), Dreamstime (Jlwhaley), Getty Images (David A. Harvey/National Geographic, Melissa Farlow, Popperfoto, Harrison Shull, Tyrone Turner/National Geographic), iStockphoto (William Britten, Steve Byland)

Library of Congress Cataloging-in-Publication Data
Wimmer, Teresa, 1975–
North Carolina / by Teresa Wimmer.
p. cm. — (This land called America)
Includes bibliographical references and index.
ISBN 978-1-58341-786-7
1. North Carolina—Juvenile literature. I. Title. II. Series.
F254.3.W56 2009
975.6—dc22   2008009515

First Edition
9 8 7 6 5 4 3 2 1

This Land Called America

NORTH CAROLINA

Teresa Wimmer

North Carolina

TERESA WIMMER

ON A PLEASANT SUMMER DAY, HIKERS TREK
HIGH INTO THE BLUE RIDGE MOUNTAINS.
WHEN THEY REACH THE TOP OF ONE OF THE
PEAKS, THEY LOOK OUT OVER MILES AND MILES
OF TREE-COVERED SLOPES. BELOW THEM,
PEOPLE KAYAK DOWN THE COOL, CLEAR WATERS
OF THE SAVANNAH RIVER. FARTHER AHEAD,
BRAVE WHITEWATER RAFTERS RIDE THE RUSHING
RAPIDS. THE HIKERS STOP AND SET UP A PICNIC
ON A GRASSY AREA, THE CRASHING SOUNDS
OF A WATERFALL IN THE BACKGROUND. AS
THEY BREATHE IN THE CLEAN, FRESH AIR, THEY
CANNOT WAIT TO ENJOY ALL OF THE OTHER
OUTDOOR ACTIVITIES NORTH CAROLINA HAS
TO OFFER.

YEAR
1540 Spanish explorer Hernando de Soto searches western North Carolina for gold.
EVENT

Road to Statehood

Long ago, American Indian tribes such as the Moratok, Pamlico, Hatteras, Catawba, and Cherokee inhabited the land that now makes up North Carolina. Eventually, the Cherokee became the largest tribe in the area. The Cherokee were taller and stronger than the other tribes and

traveled far from their villages to hunt deer, bears, wild turkeys, and other animals.

Men from Spain and Italy explored North Carolina's coast
in the early 1500s. But they did not settle there. In 1585, English
statesman Sir Walter Raleigh funded the voyage of 108 people
to sail from England to North Carolina. Those people founded
the first English colony in North America on Roanoke Island
and built Fort Raleigh there, but all returned to England the
following year. A second colony was started in 1587, but
those people mysteriously disappeared by 1590.

The first permanent white settlers in North Carolina were
English and came from Virginia. In the 1650s, they moved into
the Albermarle Sound area in the northeastern part of the

*Cherokee women
made traditional
styles of pottery
(opposite) long before
English settlers arrived
in Sir Walter Raleigh's
(above) ships.*

YEAR

1585 Settlers sent by Sir Walter Raleigh establish Roanoke Island, the first English colony in North America.

EVENT

- 7 -

state. Soon, more European immigrants came to the new land. They traded clothing and metals with the Indians for furs and tobacco. The Indians taught the settlers how to grow crops such as corn, beans, tobacco, and squash in the fertile soil.

In 1663, England's King Charles II gave eight wealthy Englishmen control over a large area of land that included North Carolina. Eventually, the settlers in North Carolina began to resent being ruled by the English. In 1775, they joined the 12 other American colonies in fighting for the right to govern themselves in the Revolutionary War. When the war ended in 1783, the colonies gained their independence from England. On November 21, 1789, North Carolina became the 12th state to join the new United States.

Throughout the 1800s, people continued immigrating to North Carolina. They came from Italy, Germany, England, Scotland, Ireland, and all over the U.S. They hoped to get rich by mining, trading, fishing, or farming. In 1803, gold was found in large quantities for the first time in the U.S. at Reed Gold Mine near Charlotte.

Tobacco and cotton soon became North Carolina's most important crops. The men who grew these crops became very wealthy. They owned large plantations, which consisted of huge homes and thousands of acres of land. Many Africans

Established in 1710, New Bern is the second-oldest town in the state and escaped harm during the Civil War.

YEAR

1655   Nathaniel Batts becomes the first European man to permanently settle in North Carolina.

EVENT

- 9 -

were captured and brought to plantations in North Carolina and other Southern states to work as slaves.

By the 1860s, many of the Northern states wanted to end slavery. But the 11 Southern states did not. One by one, they separated from the Northern states throughout 1861. The North and the South then fought against each other in the Civil War. When the war ended in 1865, all of the slaves were set free. Many of them then worked in North Carolina's tobacco and cotton fields for pay.

In the late 1800s, more and more people came to North Carolina. Mills that turned cotton into clothing and wood into paper sprang up along the state's rivers. People also built factories that used hardwood trees such as oaks and maples to make lumber for furniture. Many farmers moved to the cities to work in these factories and mills. By 1900, the state was at the beginning of a new industrial age.

In the early 1900s, many freed African Americans still picked cotton in the fields (above), and children staffed the mills in the state (opposite).

YEAR

1663   England's King Charles II grants the land that would become North Carolina to eight Englishmen.

EVENT

- 10 -

Mountains and Seashore

North Carolina lies in the South Atlantic region along the eastern coast of the U.S. To the north, the state of Virginia borders North Carolina, and South Carolina lies along its southern edge. Tennessee touches North Carolina's western border, and Georgia touches its southwestern corner. The Atlantic Ocean forms the state's eastern boundary.

The land that makes up North Carolina can be thought of as being on a downhill slope from left to right, or from west to east. The state can be divided into three main land regions: the Mountain Region in the west, the Piedmont Plateau in the middle, and the Atlantic Coastal Plain in the east.

Ranges of the ancient Appalachian Mountains, including the Blue Ridge and Great Smoky mountains, make up the western Mountain Region of North Carolina. Thousands of pine trees line the slopes of the Blue Ridge Mountains. The trees give off a natural chemical that makes the mountains look hazy blue. Mount Mitchell, a Blue Ridge peak that rises to 6,684 feet (2,037 m), is the highest point in the state and the tallest peak of the Appalachians.

The Appalachian Mountains contain some very valuable and beautiful rocks. Rubies, sapphires, kyanite, moonstones, garnets, and other stones are found throughout the mountain ranges. Small amounts of crushed stone, phosphate rock, sand, and gravel are also mined from North Carolina's mountains.

North Carolina offers views of the ocean from the shore (above) and the Blue Ridge Mountains from Mount Mitchell (opposite).

YEAR

1705   The first town in North Carolina is built by English settlers at Bath.

EVENT

- 13 -

To the east of the Mountain Region, the land drops off in an area known as the Piedmont Plateau. The point where the land drops sharply is known as the Fall Line. When rivers flow over this line, they often form crashing waterfalls. Upper Whitewater Falls, on the Whitewater River, drops 411 feet (125 m). It is one of the highest waterfalls in the eastern half of the U.S.

The Piedmont is a patchwork land of red clay soil and green fields growing tobacco and sweet potatoes. Most people in North Carolina live on farms and in small cities in this region. Many of the state's largest cities—including Charlotte, Greensboro, Winston-Salem, and the state capital of Raleigh—are found in this area. Lake Norman, North Carolina's largest lake, is also located there. It has 520 miles (837 km) of shoreline.

From downtown Raleigh's grand, granite capitol (above) to the majestic Upper Whitewater Falls of the southwest (opposite), the state offers many impressive sights.

1789   North Carolina becomes the 12th state in America on November 21.

*The swirling sandbars
beneath the water
surrounding the Outer
Banks can be plainly
seen from the air.*

The largest region in North Carolina is the Atlantic Coastal Plain. It covers 45 percent of the state. Most of the land there is flat and swampy. The Great Dismal Swamp in the northeastern corner of the state is covered with black gum and cypress trees. Birds such as pheasants and ducks, animals such as foxes and beavers, and rare plants such as Venus flytraps live there.

Hurricanes that begin in the Atlantic Ocean can adversely affect the entire eastern part of the state.

The Outer Banks is a string of islands that run along the eastern coast of North Carolina. The islands stretch in a 200-mile (320 km) line that looks like a boot along the coast. They help protect the mainland from hurricanes.

People in North Carolina often see extreme weather. In the summer, the temperature can reach 100 °F (38 °C), and in the winter, it can drop below 0 °F (-18 °C). Each year, North Carolina gets 40 to 80 inches (102–203 cm) of precipitation, both rain and snow. In the spring and summer, tornadoes often blow through. About once every four years, a tropical storm or hurricane strikes the North Carolina coast.

YEAR
1799 The first gold nugget in the U.S. is found in a creek on John Reed's farm in Cabarrus County.
EVENT

A Mixed Bag

COUNTRY LIVING HAS ALWAYS BEEN IMPORTANT TO NORTH CAROLINIANS. ABOUT ONE-THIRD OF THE STATE'S PEOPLE LIVE IN RURAL AREAS AND SMALL TOWNS. BACK-ROADS DINERS SERVE BOTH LOCALS AND TOURISTS NORTH CAROLINA FAVORITES SUCH AS GRITS, FRIED CATFISH, AND SWEET POTATO PIE.

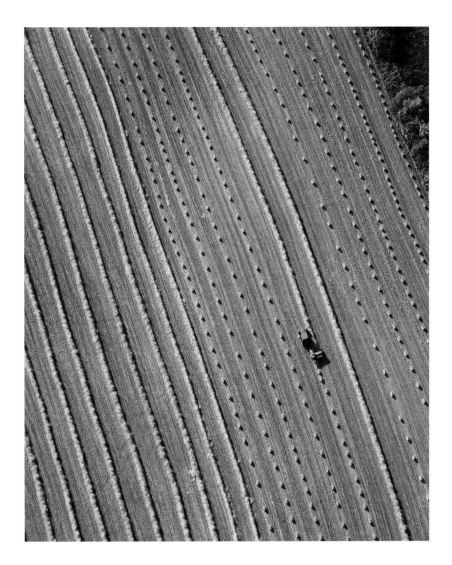

North Carolina is one of the fastest-growing states in the U.S. From 2000 to 2006, its population increased by about 10 percent. About 70 percent of the state's population is white, and about 20 percent is African American. A small but growing number of North Carolinians are of Asian and Hispanic descent. American Indians also live in the state, but their numbers are much lower than when the first Europeans arrived in the 1500s.

At first, most North Carolinians farmed. They grew corn, cotton, and tobacco in the rich soil. In the late 1800s, a man named Washington Duke began growing and harvesting

Fried catfish is a popular dinner for many Southerners (opposite), but North Carolina farm animals eat hay harvested by farmers (above).

Tobacco leaves are hung up to dry in large sheds as part of a process called curing.

tobacco on a small piece of land. By the early 1900s, the Duke family had become very wealthy from growing tobacco and manufacturing tobacco products. In 1924, the family donated millions of dollars to help fund Duke University and three other colleges in the Carolinas.

Today, about 20 percent of North Carolinians still farm. Many farmers raise broiler chickens, turkeys, ducks, and dairy cattle. They ship their products to stores around the country. In eastern North Carolina, farmers grow soybeans and corn. In the Piedmont, fields of sweet potatoes and peanuts cover the rolling hills. Even though smoking is not as popular today as it used to be, tobacco is still an important crop in North Carolina. Factories in Greensboro, Reidsville, and Winston-Salem help North Carolina produce more cigarettes, pipe tobacco, and chewing tobacco than any other state.

The design of Duke University's chapel was based on the wishes of James B. Duke, son of Washington Duke.

YEAR

1889 The U.S. government establishes a reservation for the Cherokee in western North Carolina.

EVENT

The Research Triangle Park houses about 150 companies in comfortable, spacious buildings.

North Carolina also leads all other states in making furniture. High Point, in the western part of the state, is called the "Furniture Capital of the World." More than 120 factories in the area make fine oak, hemlock, sycamore, pine, and hickory furniture for every room in the home.

Many people who live in the triangle of land between Raleigh, Chapel Hill, and Durham are employed at the Research Triangle Park, which is in the center of the triangle. This is the largest research park in the U.S., and more than 40,000 scientists, engineers, and computer technicians research new and better products there. North Carolina is also home to eight of the country's most important military bases, including Fort Bragg, Cherry Point Air Station, and Seymour Johnson Air Force Base.

Since 1911, the Hickory Chair Company has been making furniture such as dining room chairs.

YEAR
1903   Orville and Wilbur Wright complete the world's first successful airplane flight at Kitty Hawk.
EVENT

- 23 -

Tuna fisherman

North Carolina's shoreline has always provided people with many work opportunities. Each year, fishermen at the state's ports bring in about 90,000 tons (81,650 t) of shrimp, flounder, and clams from the ocean. Ships from all over the world dock at the ports of Wilmington and Morehead City to pick up goods and transport them to other places.

One place along the shore became important to the future of world transportation at the beginning of the 20th century. In 1900, brothers Orville and Wilbur Wright came from Ohio to the North Carolina coast to test their new invention: the airplane. They chose North Carolina because of its high winds. In 1903, they took off from Kitty Hawk, on the Outer Banks, and stayed in the air for 12 seconds in the world's first successful airplane flight. The brothers returned to Kitty Hawk several times to test later models.

The Outer Banks, long known for its excellent fishing waters (above), is also remembered as the site of the Wright brothers' early flights from Kitty Hawk (opposite).

A school for Cherokee Indians in Robeson County changes its name to Pembroke State College for Indians.

Hardwoods and Back Roads

North Carolina's natural wonders provide visitors and residents alike with many opportunities to enjoy the outdoors. In the summer, people enjoy boating, fishing, whitewater rafting, golfing, and tennis. In the winter, the mountain snows provide good conditions for skiing and snowboarding.

Visitors also enjoy driving and hiking the many trails along North Carolina's western mountains. The Blue Ridge Parkway is a 469-mile-long (755 km) scenic highway that winds through the Appalachians in North Carolina and Virginia. Drivers on this road can look out over stunning rivers and valleys far below.

For those searching for city life in the mountains, Asheville is North Carolina's largest mountain city. Located in the Blue Ridge Mountains, this city of approximately 69,000 is home to the Biltmore estate, a grand mansion built for multimillionaire George W. Vanderbilt in 1895. Each year, thousands of visitors tour Biltmore's 250 rooms and enjoy its nearly 70 acres (28 ha) of beautiful flower gardens.

Farther east, visitors to Greensboro can reflect on some of North Carolina's more recent history. Greensboro was the site of the nation's first protests against the segregation, or forced separation, of whites and blacks. In 1960, four black students sat down at a lunch counter for whites only in a Woolworth's store there. They refused to leave, even though they were never served. Their protest was called a sit-in. Four chairs from the Woolworth's lunch counter can be seen at the Greensboro Historical Museum.

About 60 miles (97 km) east of the impressive Biltmore estate (above) are scenic golfing opportunities near Linville (opposite).

YEAR

1960   Peaceful protests against segregation spread nationwide following the Greensboro sit-ins.

EVENT

- 27 -

The spiral-striped Cape Hatteras Lighthouse has earned the nickname "The Big Barber Pole."

In the southwestern part of the state, Charlotte is home to other educational opportunities, including Discovery Place. Visitors to this hands-on activity center can tour a science museum and touch a man-made tornado. They can even explore a rainforest habitat, complete with waterfalls and exotic birds.

North Carolina is home to its share of wild animals, especially at Asheboro's North Carolina Zoological Park. This is the country's largest walk-through natural habitat zoo. Visitors can walk the five miles (8 km) of trails through the Uwharrie Mountains to see gorillas, giraffes, polar bears, zebras, and many other animals in replicas of their natural settings.

Each summer, thousands of tourists flock to the sunny beaches along North Carolina's shoreline. Some of them take ferry rides to the Outer Banks. The famous Cape Hatteras Lighthouse at Cape Point is one of the most photographed sights in the country. At 208 feet (63 m), it is the tallest brick lighthouse in the U.S. Its black and white stripes can be seen from miles away.

Along with all of its attractions, North Carolina also offers plenty of sporting action. Four of the country's leading college basketball teams can be found at the University of North Carolina, Duke University, North Carolina State University,

The basketball rivalry between Duke and the University of North Carolina is one of college sports' fiercest.

YEAR
1989   Hurricane Hugo slams into the North Carolina coast, causing flooding and damage as far inland as Charlotte.
EVENT

- 28 -

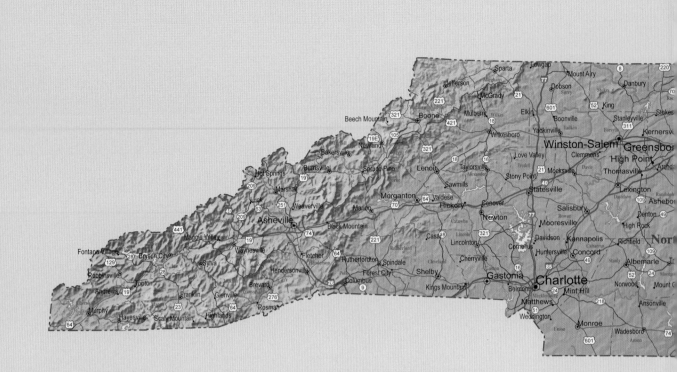

QUICK FACTS

Population: 9,061,032

Largest city: Charlotte (pop. 671,588)

Capital: Raleigh

Entered the union: November 21, 1789

Nicknames: Tar Heel State, Old North State

State flower: flowering dogwood

State bird: cardinal

Size: 53,819 sq mi (139,391 sq km)—28th-biggest in U.S.

Major industries: fishing, farming, manufacturing, tourism

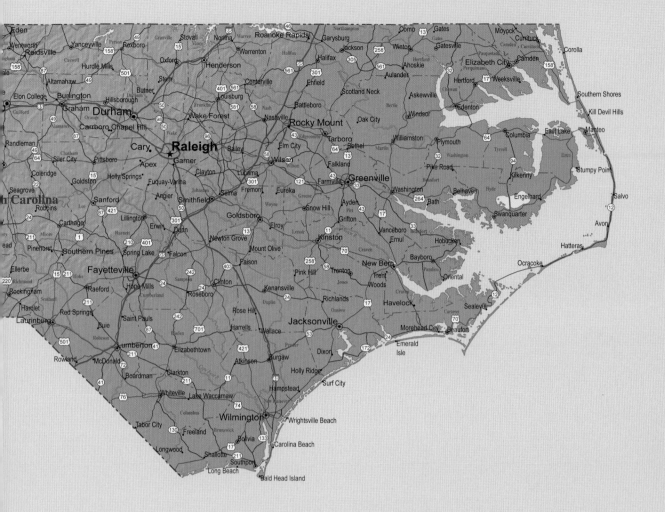

and Wake Forest University. Fans also cheer for North Carolina's professional sports teams, including football's Carolina Panthers, hockey's Carolina Hurricanes, and basketball's Charlotte Bobcats.

North Carolinians take pride in their state's clear, blue waters, rolling farmland, and majestic mountains. Many residents find time to enjoy a glass of lemonade on the front porch, fish in a nearby river, or take a stroll through the countryside. As North Carolina's population and industry continue to grow, North Carolinians strive to preserve the Southern charm for which their state has long been known.

YEAR
2006 *Site Selection* magazine names North Carolina as the top state in the U.S. for business development.
EVENT

BIBLIOGRAPHY

Explore North Carolina. "Homepage." North Carolina Department of Commerce. http://www.visitnc.com.

Mobil Travel Guide. *Coastal Southeast 2006*. Lincolnwood, Ill.: ExxonMobil Travel Publications, 2006.

Porter, Darwin, and Danforth Prince. *Frommer's The Carolinas and Georgia*. Hoboken, N.J.: Wiley Publishing, 2007.

Publications Division. "The 2006 North Carolina Manual." North Carolina Department of the Secretary of State. http://www.secretary.state.nc.us/pubsweb/manual.aspx.

Sigalas, Mike. *Moon Handbooks*: *North Carolina*. Emeryville, Calif.: Avalon Travel, 2003.

INDEX